Joe Mendoza

Bay Area Rail Transit Album Vol. 3
Caltrain
All 32 Stations in Full Color

www.metrocitybooks.com
San Francisco
2015

Dedicated to my father, Donald Mendoza.

Photographs copyright ©2015 by Joe Mendoza, unless otherwise noted.
Text copyright ©2015 by Joe Mendoza
Maps by Joe Mendoza
ISBN-13:978-1505302325
ISBN-10:1505302323
Published by www.metrocitybooks.com
P.O. Box 31635
San Francisco, California 94131-0635
Visit us at www.metrocitybooks.com

Thanks to Jack Tillmany for the use of photos from his extensive collection, and to Terry Wade and Ken Moore for all their help.

Courtesy of Santa Clara City Library Heritage Pavilion

Santa Clara station surrounded by farmlands in the early 20th century; this area is now in the center of Silicon Valley.

Cover photos:
Top: Fouth & King, San Francisco
Bottom Left: San Jose Dirodon
Bottom Right: San Bruno

Frontispiece: Three trains are ready to depart the San Francisco Caltrain station early on the morning of April 16, 2013.

Contents

The San Francisco & San Jose Rail Road; and the origin of the Southern Pacific Railroad

The origin of the railroad that became Caltrain reaches back to 1851 when the "Pacific and Atlantic Rail Road" was organized. The road's backers had the grand ambition of building a trans-continental railroad, but could not attract enough investors. In 1859 the PARR was re-organized as the "San Francisco and San Jose Rail Road Company." and its ambitions were scaled back to match the name change; however, the company still could not raise enough capital to begin construction. Finally, in April 1861, the counties of San Francisco, San Mateo, and Santa Clara, in anticipation of the economic advantages that a railroad would bring, committed $600,000 to build the railroad.

The railroad began construction at San Franciscito (Little San Francisco) Creek on the border between Santa Clara and San Mateo Counties in May 1861. Only four towns were along the original line: San Francisco at the north end; the much smaller San Jose and nearby Santa Clara at the south end ; the very small town of Redwood City was about halfway between San Francisco and San Jose.

The largest obstacle on the proposed route was Mount San Bruno, just to the south of San Francisco. The mountain's steep slopes prevented easy access to the city along the shore of the bay, so the railroad was built to the west along the "Oceanview" route.

The line then ran through San Francisco's Mission District, cutting across streets every couple of hundred yards, and at times running in streets (including Harrison Street). The "Oceanview" route contained sharp curves and steep grades (up to a 3% slope, the maximum possible for steel wheels on steel rails). Helper engines were required at the steepest grade over Oceanview Summit, just south of the San Francisco County line near where the Daly City BART Station was later built (the BART route, south of 24th & Mission, follows the Southern Pacific's former Oceanview line).

In October 1863 passenger service began between 19th & Valencia Streets in San Francisco and Mayfield, now California Avenue in Palo Alto (at the time Mayfield was a separate community). Scheduled stops included San Miguel, San Bruno, 17 Mile House (Millbrae), San Mateo, Belmont, Redwood City and Menlo Park. January 16, 1864, saw the extension of passenger service to a brick terminal building, constructed at San Pedro Street in San Jose. On February 13, 1864, the line was extended to 16th and Harrison in San

The Santa Clara Station, built in 1863, is the oldest passenger station in California.

The Southern Pacific Depot at San Jose, Cal.

Postcard from 1916, showing the 1886 Southern Pacific Railroad depot at San Jose. This replaced the earlier San Francisco & San Jose depot, opened in 1864.

Francisco, and then along temporary rails laid in the middle of Brannon Street to a temporary station at Fourth and Brannon. After the filling of Mission Bay in 1869, the San Francisco Terminal was moved to Fourth & Townsend, and six years later it moved to a new structure at Third & Townsend.

The managers of the San Francisco and San Jose Rail Road incorporated the Southern Pacific Railroad in 1865. The US Congress granted the Southern Pacific the rights to create a southern transcontinental railroad from San Francisco south to San Diego and then east to New Orleans. The route was soon revised to run east from what was then the small village of Los Angeles.

The Menlo Park Station, built in 1867, is the second oldest passenger station in California. Menlo Park and Santa Clara are the only surviving stations built by the San Francisco & San Jose Rail Road.

The owners of the Southern Pacific (the managers of the San Francisco and San Jose Rail Road) purchased the stock that the counties of San Francisco, San Mateo and Santa Clara owned, ending the first short period of public ownership in March, 1868. It would be over a hundred years before the line became public property again.

The SP began construction south of San Jose towards Gilroy in April, 1868. This part of the SP route was built under the authority of the "Santa Clara & Pajaro Valley Rail Road Company." From Gilroy the SP built two separate branches; the branch to the town of Tres Pinos was to cross the Coast Range and run down the San Joaquin Valley to Los Angeles, and the other branch was to follow the coast though Salinas, San Luis Obispo, and Santa Barbara.

Meanwhile, the Central Pacific and Union Pacific Railroads had completed the first transcontinental railroad from Omaha, Nebraska to Oakland, California. The Central Pacific Railroad, the owners of the western half of that route, wanted to prevent competition to their expensive investment, and by September, 1868, they had gained control of the upstart Southern Pacific.

The independent identity of the San Francisco and San Jose Rail Road ended in 1870 when it was absorbed into the Southern Pacific, although the Central Pacific and the SP (now owned by the CP) remained separate companies. The Central Pacific extended its tracks down the San Joaquin Valley to where the Southern Pacific had been granted the right to construct its railroad. With the connection to the CP, the route from Tres Pinos, over what would have been a difficult crossing of the Coast Range, was never completed. The Coast Route was also delayed, and would not be completed until 1901.

In 1883 the Southern Pacific's transcontinental line was completed and quickly became the CP/SP's most profitable route. The Southern Pacific route was fully owned by the Central Pacific, and therefore, the CP did not have to share profits with another railroad, as it did with the Union Pacific over the original transcontinental. Also, the southern route crossed lower mountains than did the original route, this, along with the more southern latitude, meant that the route was open during winter months when the more northerly route was blocked by snow.

A new holding company was formed in 1885 to operate all the railroads under the Central Pacific's control. The new company, the Southern Pacific Company, was named for the most profitable part of its operations. The Central Pacific's name disappeared.

The station at Valencia and 19th in San Francisco was the SF&SJRR's first terminal in San Francisco. Note its similarity to the Santa Clara Station (pg 4 & pg 68), also built by the SF&SJRR. Even after the railroad was extended beyond Valencia Street it remained an important way-station. However the station's importance rapidly declined after the completion of the Bayshore cutoff in 1907. The last passenger train stopped at the station in 1930 and the last freight train passed by in 1942.

San Francisco History Center,
San Francisco Public Library

The Southern Pacific and the Peninsula Commute

Passenger service between San Francisco and San Jose began with two trips a day in each direction. By 1890, service had increased to three trips between San Francisco and Menlo Park and another four trains between San Francisco and San Jose, plus several long distance trains that continued south and east of San Jose.

The number of passenger trains on the single-tracked railroad had increased to 29 a day by 1901. This route also carried numerous freight trains heading for the yard at 16th & Mariposa in San Francisco. In 1889 the Southern Pacific announced its intention to double-track the route from San Jose to San Francisco. South of San Bruno, the Southern Pacific met with no opposition; and that part of the route was double-tracked by 1897. In the heavily congested Mission District of San Francisco, where railroad tracks crossed city streets every couple of hundred feet, the announcement was met with fierce resistance from the residents and businesses. The possibility of double tracking the original route became politically untenable after city officials joined with the residents and businesses in opposition to the plans. The Southern Pacific needed to find another way to enter the city in a method acceptable to the people of San Francisco.

The Southern Pacific had investigated rerouting the line to the shore of the San Francisco Bay in 1873. The advantages of the route had been numerous. It would be three miles shorter than the inland route, and the curvature would be reduced from a maximum of 12 degrees to just 4 degrees. The route would be practically level, with a maximum of a 0.3% slope. However, the cost would be extraordinary. The required cutting and filling and the necessary trestles and tunnels brought the costs up to a million dollars a mile (approximately 100 million dollars a mile in today's prices). However, after the option of double tracking the Oceanview route was blocked, the SP decided that it had no choice; it had to build the new line along the bay's shore.

In 1904, construction of the Bay Shore cutoff began (the name of the cutoff, originally referred to as "Bay Shore," was soon changed to Bayshore"). The cutoff included five tunnels (four still used) and a great deal of landfill. A temporary trestle was built over Visitacion Bay, a cove between Candlestick Point on the southern border of San Francisco and Visitacion Point. Excavated materials from tunnels and cuts, along with material dredged from the bay, were used to fill Visitacion Bay.

A large freight terminal was built on the filled land. The terminal added much needed capacity to San Francisco. The Bayshore yard was 8400 feet long, and it included a round house, a car shop and a hump. A "hump" is a small hill from where cars can be rolled via gravity to a classification bowl where they are sorted. Before the Bayshore yard was built, the only SP yard with a hump was at Roseville in the Sierra foothills. The old freight yard, at 16th & Mariposa, with its round house and car shop, was closed after the new yard opened in 1907.

The route was built to be easily expanded to four tracks. With the coming of High Speed Rail, more than a century after the cutoff was built; this excess capacity may soon be used. Four of the five tunnels along the cutoff (three of the four presently used) were only built for two tracks, but tunnel #2, was built for four tracks.

Associated with this huge undertaking was a project to create a short cut from the East Bay, at Niles (now part of Fremont) to Redwood City. Previously, all direct traffic from the north and east of San Francisco (that didn't cross the bay by barge) had to travel south to San Jose before returning north to San Francisco. The Southern Pacific built a new eleven mile line from Niles, through Newark, to Dumbarton Point on the bay. SP then built the first bridge across the bay, crossing from Dumbarton Point to East Palo Alto; from there the SP built a new line to Redwood City. On September 12, 1910, the Dumbarton cutoff was opened.

This line (presently unused) is the route of the proposed Dumbarton Rail, a new commuter line between the BART station at Union City and the Caltrain station at Redwood City. The proposed service would split at Redwood City, with half the trains continuing north to San Francisco and half turning south to Silicon Valley and San Jose.

The Bayshore project was almost complete when the Great San Francisco Earthquake of 1906 struck. The SP headquarters at Fourth and Townsend burned and much of the rails over the Oceanview line were twisted. Several bridges along the Peninsula line shifted off their foundations. Tunnels #2 and #5 on the new Bayshore cutoff collapsed.

The tunnels were rebuilt and the Bayshore cutoff was opened on December 7, 1907. All through

Tunnel Number 2, just to the north of the Bayshore Station is seen here in a photo from the early 1900's. See page 25 for a present day view of the same area.

Much of the debris from the great earthquake of 1906 was removed from San Francisco via the Southern Pacific.

traffic was removed from the Oceanview line, leaving only local traffic. Seventeen minutes were removed from the scheduled travel time from the towns south of San Bruno to San Francisco. The old single-tracked route was served by loop trains that ran down to Tanforan (near San Bruno) by one route and returned by the other (see pg. 28).

After the great Earthquake of 1906, refugees from San Francisco fled south, settling in San Mateo County. The settlement of the Peninsula was spurred on in part by the quicker and more intensive service made possible by the double tracking of the line and by the shorter route provided by the Bayshore Cutoff. The Peninsula's population boomed, along with the SP's commute business. Commute trains (at Southern Pacific they were always commute trains, not commuter trains) were streaming into San Francisco in the morning and streaming out in the evening.

In 1915, a new passenger station was completed at Third & Townsend to serve the crowds arriving for the 1915 Panama Pacific Exposition. It was to have been a temporary station. The SP wanted to extend the track further into San Francisco to a station across from the Ferry Building at the foot of Market Street. But this was never completed, and the temporary station survived until 1975

Thirty-four daily commute round trips were running between San Jose and San Francisco by 1925, along with numerous long distance passenger trains and freight trains. In 1921, the Southern Pacific's chief engineer George Boschke commissioned a report on the feasibility of electrifying the line between San Jose and San Francisco, along with triple-tracking the line from Redwood City (where the Dumbarton Cutoff fed into the peninsula line) to San Bruno and four-tracking the line from San Bruno into San Francisco. Boschke also looked at the possibility of extending the electrified line in a subway under Eighth Street to a new underground station at the Civic Center. SP decided that the benefits of electrification were not worth the costs. The SP, however, did buy land next to its right-of-way from San Mateo to Redwood City, but they never added the extra track. In 1942, the Oceanview line was cut back to Daly City and tracks were removed from the outer Mission district. The last passenger service on the Oceanview line was abandoned at the same time.

The commute trains reached a peak of popularity during World War II. After the war, housing developments and shopping malls began to sprawl across the Peninsula. A small decline in the passenger count followed the War, but the decline quickly turned around and passenger counts continued to rise until reaching its pre-Caltrain peak of 16,000 per day in 1955. The SP's commute trains became longer (up to 17 cars) and were extending beyond the platforms. To cope with the crowds the SP bought its first 10 bi-level gallery cars (based on the design of Chicago's bi-level commuter rail coaches) and placed them in service in June and July 1955. The new cars successfully increased passenger accommodations without increasing train length; so, SP ordered another 21 gallery cars in 1956.

Southern Pacific began converting from steam power to diesel power after World War II. The first diesels on the Peninsula commute were run on September 28, 1953; although most commute runs remained steam hauled. By 1956, all of the Southern Pacific had been dieselized, with the exception of the Peninsula Commute Service, which continued to be run with steam engines bumped from other parts of the SP Empire. However, steam would soon be gone from the Peninsula. The last steam run on the entire Southern Pacific system (with the exception of an occasional excursion) came on January 22, 1957, when train number 146 left San Francisco at 5:45 PM for its one hour and 50 minute run to San Jose.

The first diesels on the commute had been a few GP9 locomotives (Geeps), but full dieselization came with the Fairbanks-Morse Train Masters in 1956 and 1957. The F-M Train Masters were originally built for freight service out of El Paso, but proved temperamental in the dry desert climate. The Train Masters tended to emit sparks which started fires in the dry grasses growing along its tracks. After being re-assigned to the commute service, the locomotives preformed well. By February 27, 1960, the round house at Mission Bay, used for servicing steam engines, had been closed. By 1975 all the FM Train Masters had been replaced by SDP45 diesel locomotives. The Southern Pacific leased fifteen P30CH diesel locomotives from Amtrak for the commute service in 1978.

Even though the commute service was heavily used, the Southern Pacific began to trim the schedule. Two round trips were cut in 1953, a third in 1956, and a fourth in 1957.

After 1955, freeways and automobiles began biting into the commute's customer base; a steady decrease in the SP's passenger count had begun. SP started closing Peninsula stations in 1959. Throughout the 1960's and 70's the decline continued. The SP claimed a $650,000 annual lose on the commute service by 1964. The SP was losing money, but it refused to seek public subsidies for fear of government interference. The Southern Pacific attempted to cut its losses. The SP proposed to turn 5 trains at Belmont (instead of running to San Jose) and to increase the fares by 30%. In 1964, the Los Gatos branch (Mayfield Cut-off) was abandoned and the Foothill Expressway built in its right-of-way. On a more positive note, the Southern Pacific bought 15 more gallery cars in 1968, (gallery cars are less labor intensive than the old suburban 'Harimans').

May 1, 1971, is known to rail fans as "Amtrak Day," the day that Amtrak took over most long distance passenger trains in the U.S. By April 30, 1971, only two non-Commute trains were terminating at San Francisco. On May 1, 1971, The Del Monte was discontinued and the terminal for the Coast Daylight was moved to Oakland. Long-distance passenger trains no longer traveled on the Peninsula north of Santa Clara.

Before 1971, the southern part of Santa Clara County and the northern part of Monterey County was served by the Southern Pacific's Del Monte. This name train had a morning run from Monterey to San Francisco and an evening run back to Monterey. On the eve of Amtrak, and the nationalization of long distance passenger service, the patrons of the Del Monte tried to save the train by arguing that it was a commuter run, and did not fall under the Amtrak legislation. However, the Del Monte would be the last 'non-commute' passenger run operated by the Southern Pacific when, in the evening of April 30, 1971, the Del Monte was deadheaded from Monterey to San Francisco. The California PUC (Public Utilities Commission) tried to save the Del Monte, but hearings on May 12, 1971, failed to convince the ICC (Interstate Commerce Commission). The ICC ruled that the Del Monte was not a commuter run and that the Southern Pacific was not required to re-establish the service. With the exception of Garlic Festival Specials (see pg. 86), no local passenger service would be seen on the Del Monte's route until after the earthquake of 1989.

Following the Coast Daylight's switch to Oakland, its schedule was reduced from daily to four days a week. A new un-named train was added to fill in on the other three days; the new train ran from Seattle to San Diego (later to Los Angeles). On November 14, 1971, this service was named the "Coast Starlight," north of Oakland; while south of Oakland it retained the Daylight name. The Starlight's service became daily in 1973, and the "Starlight" name was soon applied to the whole route: the "Daylight" name was retired.

Between 1968 and 1972, the Southern Pacific successfully asked the PUC for five fare increases, raising the fare 43%. The SP then asked for a 111% rate increase in August, 1973. A secret SP study was discovered which showed that a price increase of "only" 40% would lead to a passenger drop of more than 60%. The rate increase was denied. In 1975 SP offered to sell part of their right-of-way for 200 million dollars, but the offer only included one of the two tracks, and only between San Jose and San Bruno, and then the old Oceanview line as far as the Daly City BART station, where passengers would have to change to BART trains to complete their journey into San Francisco. The offer was declined.

In 1976, (after daily ridership had declined to 8000), the Southern Pacific offered a series of strange proposals, including a plan to have a fleet of eight-person vans replace the commute trains. The plans were not taken seriously by any government agency.

By 1977 the ridership had declined to 7,500 passengers per day. The Southern Pacific asked the PUC for permission to discontinue the commute service. The SP's request was refused. SP attempted to drop all but weekday rush-hour trains in February 1978, but again it was rebuffed. Finally, in May, 1980, the state of California and the counties of San Francisco, San Mateo and Santa Clara negotiated an agreement to provide not less than $250 million to upgrade the service and to underwrite the SP's deficit. The agreement operated under a 10 year renewable contract. The state service was to be named "CalTrain" (CalTrain before 1992, Caltrain after). CalTrain would be responsible for scheduling, setting fares, and for maintenance and performance standards. SP would be responsible for running the trains and for meeting the CalTrain standards.

On July 1, 1980, the State took control. CalTrain immediately began plans to increase the 22 daily round trips to 26.

Left: Tower at San Francisco. Traffic control functions were consolidated at San Jose Diridon in 1993 and the towers at San Jose Telegraph, Fourth Street San Francisco, College Park and Santa Clara were all closed.

The Decline of Freight Traffic

The freight traffic on the Peninsula route declined for a number of reasons; both geographical and technological. San Francisco is on a peninsula with a great natural harbor. The level of the bay's sea bed drops quickly on the west side of the bay and provided San Francisco with a natural deep-water port, but the east side was blocked by miles of mud flats. In California's early days, San Francisco, on the bay's western shore, became California's premier port. During those early days much of California's internal transportation, both passenger and freight, was provided by river boats. Up until World War II, most of California's agricultural product (that didn't move by rail) was moved by barge. For freight entering the bay via the river systems, it was just as convenient to dock at San Francisco as it was to dock at Oakland. But in the 1920's this began to change, most of California's non-rail interior freight began to be shipped by truck rather than water; Oakland, on the mainland provided better connections to the rest of the continent. Modern dredging techniques had created deep water ports on the bay's eastern shore. The Port of Oakland developed facilities for handling modern containerized freight, while San Francisco did not. Even for freight that was destined for San Francisco, it had become easier to ship a container to Oakland, and then to truck it across the bay.

San Francisco was also losing its manufacturing base. With the rise of the trucking industry, manufacturing plants no longer needed direct access to port facilities. As existing city factories became obsolete, many companies rebuilt in the East Bay, where land was cheaper and more abundant, and so provided greater expansion possibilities than did the tightly crowded San Francisco.

Until 1964, the Peninsula route had been part of SP's Coastal Division, with headquarters in San Francisco, and running from the city south to Santa Barbara. In 1964, the Southern Pacific's Coastal Division, north of San Luis Obispo, was consolidated with its Western Division. The Coastal Division, from San Luis Obispo south, was combined with the Los Angeles Division. Oakland, the consolidated division's operational hub, became the most important freight terminal in Northern California. During the 1960's most of the freight facilities in San Francisco were moved to Oakland.

By the 1980's the Mission Bay Yards, near downtown San Francisco, had closed, providing prime redevelopment potential. By 1988 the last freight operations at the Bayshore Yard was moved to South San Francisco. Today, South San Francisco (along with Redwood City) remains the center of the freight operations on Caltrain.

Although the number of freight trains on the Peninsula has radically declined since the days when the Peninsula was the Southern Pacific's densest freight line, several freight runs still occur in the early morning and late evenings, before and after rush hour.

South San Francisco is the center of the Peninsula's remaining freight service.

The State Takes Control

In 1980, CalTrain was created by the State of California and the counties of Santa Clara, San Mateo and San Francisco for the purpose of subsidizing SP's loses on the Commute. CalTrain would also buy new coaches and locomotives for the Commute. Early in 1980, Caltrans (California Department of Transportation) took financial and administrative responsibility for SP's Peninsula Commute (47 miles, 22 round trips per weekday) and in July of that year, the State of California began operating the Peninsula Commute. Caltrans re-branded the service as "CalTrain" and began an effort to upgrade the service. The schedules were modified in 1981 when several reverse Commute trains are added.

Under Southern Pacific control, the commute's passenger count had fallen to an all time low of 4.3 million in 1977, but then rose to 6.3 million after the county of San Mateo began to subsidize ticket prices. In 1980, the new CalTrain administration introduced a 25% fare increase and the ridership declined from 6.3 million in 1980-81 to 4.8 million in 1982-83. Southern Pacific did little to make the commute attractive, the cars were filthy. The state had to force SP to honor its obligation to keep the cars clean. Ridership then leveled off until new cars arrived in 1985 and 1986 (see below), after which ridership began to rise. Over 17 million passengers rode Caltrain in 2014.

CalTrain, during its first five years, leased Southern Pacific cars and locomotives; however, in 1985; the entire fleet was replaced with new push-pull gallery cars powered by new EMD F40's. SP had offered to sell its commute equipment to CalTrain, but Caltrans considered the price too high; the equipment was old and was not equipped for push-pull operation. On June 12, 1985, the first 20 new air conditioned cars from Japan began to appear on the commute, and the last of the Harriman Suburban Cars began to disappear. Smoking was not allowed in any of the new cars. With the new cars, and faster turn-around allowed by the push-pull technology, the commute was raised from 26 daily trips to 46. All together, 63 new cars (including 21 cab control cars) were bought from Nippon Sharyo Seizo Kaisha and Sumitomo in Japan. The cars were assembled in San Francisco at Pier 50 by General Electric with 51%+ American made parts to qualify for the "Buy American" requirement for federal funding. These gallery-type cars originally seated 139 in cab cars and 148 in the others. The last of SP's old gallery cars were gone by February, 1986. Eighteen new locomotives were built in Illinois by Electro-Motive Division of General Motors for the new push-pull trains.

After the new cars arrived in 1985 and 1986, the route's ridership began to rise again. In October 1985, CalTrain added five new daily "reverse-commute" trains for Silicon Valley workers. Service increased from 46 to 52 trains per day in 1986.

On February 25, 1981, the state gave Caltrans permission to purchase 23 of the 27 stations on the Commute this was later increased to all 25 of the Southern Pacific owned stations. The San Mateo and Millbrae Stations were already municipally owned (the present Millbrae station is owned by BART). The tracks remained part of SP.

During the 1980's the State provided half of the Commute's subsidies, but in early 1987 the pro-highway administration of Governor Deukmejian announced that it wanted to pull out of the rail commuter business by 1990. In response, "The Peninsula Commute ad hoc Joint Powers Authority" was formed by the three counties of San Francisco, San Mateo and Santa Clara. The State agreed to participate with the Joint

Powers Authority in the negotiations with SP. In June 1990, California State voters approved a $1.99 billion rail bond act that included $120 million for the purchase of the CalTrain right-of-way.

In January 1991, the Joint Powers Board agreed to purchase the 51.4 miles between San Francisco and San Jose, with provisions for future purchases of Dumbarton line (11 miles) and 8.4 miles of the Vasona branch (formerly part of the South Pacific Coast RR from San Jose to Los Gatos). CalTrain also indicated its desire to buy trackage rights for the 25 miles between San Jose and Gilroy. However talks with Southern Pacific bogged down over price and extent of

In 1995 Caltrain became Handicap accessible, trains were retrofitted and wheelchair lifts added at 15 stations.

The Caltrain logo was adopted in 1997.

the purchase, and in October, SP threatened to shut down the commute if the JPB didn't buy the route. Finally, on December 27, 1991, the PCSJPB purchased the 51.4 miles of right-of-way from Southern Pacific. Part of the agreement included an option to buy the Dumbarton Bridge. After 127 years, the line between San Francisco and San Jose returned to the ownership of the three counties that had originally financed its construction. The Dumbarton line was later purchased by the State and San Mateo County. The Vasona branch was purchased by the VTA (Santa Clara Valley Transit Authority) and is now part of the VTA light rail system.

The Commute was known as "CalTrain" (with a capital "T") from 1980 to 1990. After the State of California ended its subsidies; the Commute was referred to as "Caltrain" (small "t").

On July 1, 1992, the PCSJPB became the Peninsula Corridor Joint Power Board (PCJPB), usually referred to as the JPB. On January 15, 1992, official ceremonies were held at the historic San Carlos station to mark the $220 million purchase of the 51.4 miles of route between San Francisco and San Jose (the 47 miles of SP's Commute Route + 4.4 miles beyond the San Jose Station to Tamien). Track rights for another 25.4 miles down to Gilroy were also purchased from the SP. The SP agreed to continue running the trains along its traditional 47 mile route until another operator could be found. On June 27, 1992, Amtrak assumed the operating contact from Southern Pacific; after 129 years, the SP was no longer running passengers into San Francisco. Concurrent with Amtrak control, the service expanded from 54 to 60 weekday trips. Tamien Station (where riders could transfer from the VTA light rails) opened in San Jose and two morning and evening runs were extended to Gilroy. Presently (2015) Gilroy sees three morning departures and three evening arrivals.

In 1992, Caltrain began to allow bicycles on its trains. In 1995 all cab cars were retrofitted to carry both passengers and a minimum of 24 bikes. The Gallery Cab Cars have since been retrofitted to carry 40 bicycles. The cab cars in the newer Bombardier car originally carried 16 bikes; they have been retrofitted to allow 24. By 2011, additional cars were retrofitted to carry bikes: as of 2012, all trains carry a minimum of 2 bicycle cars allowing 80 bikes on the Nippon Sharyo Seizo Kaisha and Sumitomo trains, and 48 bikes on the Bombardier trains (see pg 14). Beginning in 2016, after a third car is added to the Bombardier trains, they will allow 72 bikes.

In 2002, Bombardier low-level-boarding cars begin to arrive for the planned CTX (Caltrain Express) service. New four-tracked bypasses were constructed at Sunnyvale and Bay Shore to allow expresses to overtake and pass locals. In 2003, new streamlined locomotives arrived. The express service was informally referred to as the Baby Bullet. By 2004, the CTX was officially re-branded as "Baby Bullet" and in June, 2004, "Baby Bullet" service began.

In 2008, Caltrain reached a record high of 98 trains per day. But by 2010, Caltrain faced financial difficulties as local and state levels of support were cut back. Caltrain threatened to eliminate weekend service and all service south of Tamien. Mid-day and evening trains were cut back from every 30 minutes to every hour, but the more draconian cuts were avoided. By 2012, the economic situation had improved and some of the eliminated trains were restored.

Future plans

Near future plans include extending express trains to 6 cars and extending platforms at express station as required. Future plans also include electrification of the line and extensions to the Transbay Terminal in San Francisco. Extensions to Monterey and/or Salinas are being proposed. Also proposed is a branch across the bay at Dumbarton to Fremont and Union City. In 1993, San Mateo County, along with the State of California, bought the Dumbarton Rail Bridge & line from the Southern Pacific (the line was last used by SP freight trains in 1982).

Left: Automatic ticket machine: In September 2003, Caltrain adopted "Proof-of-Payment" system. Conductors no longer sell tickets aboard trains. All passengers are now required to have a valid ticket or pass before boarding a train.
Single ride and round trip tickets can be bought from the machine.
To the left of the ticket machine is a Clipper Card validator for use with the Bay Area wide transit payment system. The Clipper Card can hold monthly passes, 8-ride tickets, or single-ride. A single-ride ticket bought with the Clipper Card is less expensive then when bought from the ticket machine.

Rolling Stock

In the early days, the trains used for the commute were made up of former long-distance, wooden, rail cars. In 1923, when E. H. Harriman was president of the Southern Pacific Railroad, the SP ordered its first purpose-built suburban cars. The high-capacity, 72-foot long steel cars were officially referred to as "Subs", but were more commonly known as "Harrimans". More orders came in 1924 & 1927. During the 1930's, 60-foot long versions of the steel Subs, (also called "Harrimans") were built to replace the remaining wooden cars. In total, SP ordered 75 Subs. The SP scrapped or sold the 60-foot cars in the 1960's. The Golden Gate Railroad Museum preserved eight 72-foot Harrimans; SP sold or scrapped the rest of the fleet in the 1980's.

The SP bought its first 10 bi-level gallery cars (based on the design of Chicago's bi-level commuter railcars) in 1955, and more in 1956 and 1968, for a total of 45. In 1985, most of these cars were rebuilt as sight-seeing cars for use in Alaska; the rest were scrapped.

Between 1985 and 1987, Caltrain bought 63 gallery-type cars from Nippon Sharyo Seizo Kaisha and Sumitomo in Japan. The new cars were assembled in San Francisco. The cars were 85 feet long, 25 feet 11 inches high, and weighed 123,000 lbs. The cars originally sat 139 in cab cars and 148 in the others. The twenty-one cab-control cars had punch-out panels for future conversion to handicap accessibility. In 2000, 14 new ADA (Americans with Disabilities Act) accessible trailers were purchased along with 6 new ADA accessible Cab Cars, so the conversion of the older cars was never required. There is at least one accessible car per train.

Eighteen new locomotives built in Illinois by Electro-Motive Division of General Motors (numbers 900- 917), arrived in 1985; GM built another 2 locomotives (numbers 918 & 919) in 1987. Three more locomotives arrived in 1998 from Boise (920-922), and another 6 from MPI in 2003 (923-928).

In 2001 and 2002, Caltrain bought 17 bi-level cars from Bombardier, 10 trailer and 7 cab cars. In 2008, Caltrain bought another 6 trailers and 2 cab cars from Bombardier. The entire Bombardier fleet is ADA accessible from low-level platforms. In 2015 Caltrain bought 16 used Bombardier cars from Los Angeles' MetroLink. These cars are being refurbished & will be used to extend the lengths of express trains.

Car Number	Car type	Builder & Year	Seating	Bikes	Notes
3800-3825	Gallery Trailer-Luggage car	Nippon Sharyo 1985	142	0	1
3825-3835	Gallery Trailer-Bicycle car	Nippon Sharyo 1985	108	40	1
3836-3841	Gallery Trailer	Nippon Sharyo 1985	148	0	1
3842-3851	Gallery Trailer	Nippon Sharyo 1987	148	0	1
3853-3865	Gallery Trailer	Nippon Sharyo 2000	122	0	2
4000-4020	Gallery Cab-Bicycle car	Nippon Sharyo 1985	107	40	3
4021-4026	Gallery Cab-Bicycle car	Nippon Sharyo 2000	82	40	2
112-116	Bi-level Cab-Bicycle car	Bombardier 2001-02	123	24	2
117-118	Bi-level Cab-Bicycle car	Bombardier 2002	139	24	2
219-226	Bi-level Trailer	Bombardier 2002	148	0	2
229-230	Bi-level Trailer	Bombardier 2002	148	0	2
119-120	Bi-level Cab-Bicycle car	Bombardier 2008	139	24	2
231-36	Bi-level Trailer	Bombardier 2008	148	0	2

Notes:
1: Rebuilt by Nippon Sharyo, 2000-2001   3: Toilet, (not ADA compliant)
2: ADA compliant, with toilet

Electromotive (GM) locomotive (1985)

MPI locomotive (2003)

Car 3826 - Gallery trailer, bike car.

Car 4025 - Cab Car, handicap accessible car/Bike car, part of the fleet purchased in 2000.

Cab car 4019 with the never-used punch-out panel, note the bike icon, all cab cars are also bike cars.

Car 3824 - Gallery trailer with luggage racks, note the luggage icon.

Car 3858 - Gallery trailer, handicap accessible, part of the accessible fleet purchased in 2000. Stairs fold out to form a wheel chair lift.

Car 3840 remains in the unmodified 1985 configuration, although it has been re-furbished.

Bombardier bicycle car.

Bombardier trailer, all Bombardier cars are wheel chair accessible from low-level platforms (pg. 35) or from mobile lifts (pg. 12).

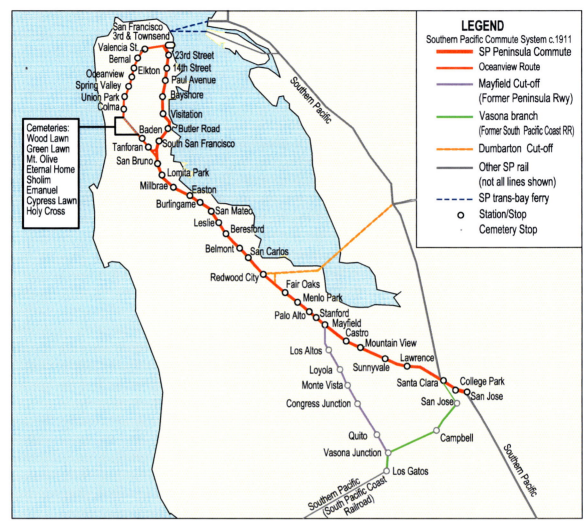

Cemeteries:
Wood Lawn
Green Lawn
Mt. Olive
Eternal Home
Sholim
Emanuel
Cypress Lawn
Holy Cross

LEGEND
Southern Pacific Commute System c.1911

━━━ SP Peninsula Commute
━━━ Oceanview Route
━━━ Mayfield Cut-off
   (Former Peninsula Rwy)
━━━ Vasona branch
   (Former South Pacific Coast RR)
━━━ Dumbarton Cut-off
━━━ Other SP rail
   (not all lines shown)
- - - SP trans-bay ferry
○   Station/Stop
·   Cemetery Stop

The Southern Pacific Commute service c. 1911

Above:The single track Oceanview route is shown between Valencia Street, in San Francisco, and Tanforan in San Bruno. Much of the Oceanview route was taken over by BART (Bay Area Rapid Transit). BART's Balboa Park Station was built next to Elkton, the Daly City BART station is located Between Oceanview and Spring Valley. BART's Colma station is near the old SP Colma Station, South San Francisco station is near Baden and BART's San Bruno station is at Tanforan. The flag stops between Woodlawn and Holy Cross were at cemeteries.

On the double tracked Bayshore cut-off, 23rd Street has been slightly relocated and renamed 22nd Street. 14th Street was been abandoned by SP. Paul Avenue was abandoned by Caltrain in 2005. The Vistacion station was abandoned by SP after World War II and the Butler Road Station was abandoned by Caltrain in the early 1980's.

The remains of the loop track between South San Francisco and the Oceanview route (see page 28) can be seen near Tanforan. In 1963, San Bruno and Lomita Park were combined into one station halfway between the two, and then relocated again in 2014.

Easton has been renamed Broadway Burlingame, Beresford is now Hillsdale, Fair Oaks is Atherton and Mayfield is California Avenue, the Castro station has been replaced with the nearby San Antonio station.

The line between Mayfield and Los Gatos (the Mayfield cut-off, originally part of the SP controlled interurban, Peninsula Railway) was abandoned in January 1964. Southern Pacific also abandoned passenger traffic on the line between San Jose and Vasona Junction. The Vasona Branch (formerly part of the South Pacific Coast Railroad, a narrow gauge line that ran from a ferry dock in Alameda to Santa Cruz, and later merged into the Southern Pacific system) is now owned by the VTA (Valley Transit Authority); Light rail has been built between San Jose and Campbell, with plans for eventual extension to Vasona Junction & Los Gatos.

San Francisco
4th & King

700 Fourth Street, San Francisco, CA 94107
Opened: 4th & Townsend (1875)
3rd & Townsend (1889/1914)
4th & King (June 21, 1975)
Mile Post 0.2 (0.3 km)

Caltrain's northern terminal is located on 4th Street between Townsend and King Streets in San Francisco. It replaced a Mission Revival station at 3rd & Townsend which was located 2/10th of a mile closer to the center of town (the mile post references used by Caltrain still refers to the Third & Townsend location). The new terminal was originally referred to as "4th & Townsend", but is now referred to as "4th & King" after the Muni-Metro light rail station was opened on the King Street side of the station. There are plans to replace this Caltrain station with an underground station when Caltrain is electrified and extended into downtown San Francisco. Some above-ground trackage will be retained for use by non-electrified trains from Gilroy or from the proposed Dumbarton connection.

The San Francisco & San Jose Rail Road originally reached San Francisco via the Oceanview line, the line that swung west of the obstruction created by Mt. San Bruno. The original terminal in San Francisco was at 19th & Valencia. In the early 1860's, the company purchased a site for a terminal at 4th and Townsend Streets. At that time, the site was still underwater in what was Mission Bay. The site was filled in by 1875, and a small wood-frame station was built at the corner of Fourth and Townsend. The reclaimed land on what had been Mission Bay was used for railroad yards. The line was later extended eastward and a much larger wood-framed station was built at Third and Townsend in 1889. In 1914, the station at Third and Townsend was replaced with a Mission Revival station.

Southern Pacific made repairs to the Third and Townsend station in 1954. The bell towers were rebuilt and the concourse roof was replaced. The City of San Francisco wanted SP to build a new station, and even threatened legal action, but SP, with its dwindling interest in passenger service, resisted the pressure, and nothing came of the threats.

From the collection of Jack Tillmany

The second station at 3rd Street between Townsend & King streets was built in 1914 at the time of San Francisco's Panama Pacific Exposition, it was to be a temporary station, but remained in use until 1972. SP had planned to expand passenger service to a station behind their corporate headquarters at Market Street and the Embarcadero, but city officials objected to bringing steam engines into the city center, and by the time diesels had replaced steam engines, SP was no longer interested in expanding passenger service.

Above: Bumper post at San Francisco. Three trains are ready for the morning reverse commute to Silicon Valley, September 13, 2011.

By 1971, the offices for the Southern Pacific, once housed in the Third Street station, had moved to Oakland. Long distance trains were removed from the terminal on May 1, 1971; commute service, although still serving 10,000 passengers a day, had declined from its peak of 18,000 per day (ridership would decline to 7,500 per day before bottoming out in 1978). Southern Pacific proposed the demolition of the San Francisco Terminal.

The approval for demolition came swiftly; in part because Caltrans (the state transportation department) coveted the land south of King Street for new off ramps for an Interstate highway. The freeway was to cut through the heart of San Francisco, but never made it beyond Third Street. the people of San Francisco were able to defeat the freeway, but the defeat came too late to save the old station.

The city of San Francisco's planning commission approved the destruction and replacement of the old station, which was quickly torn down and the site used for a recreational vehicle park until the turn of the 21st century when the area was finally re-developed.

Work began on the new, unassuming $200,000 single story building in 1973; it opened on June 21, 1975. The simple station has corrugated concrete walls, concrete columns, and a concrete waffle-slab roof. A new tower was built at 5th & Townsend, and the old tower at 4th street was demolished. In 1998, the station was remodeled and improved. The platforms were moved twenty feet to the west and a new light-filled circulation area, built of steel and glass, was inserted between the 1975 station and the platforms.

The section of the freeway, separating the Ferry Building from San Francisco's business district, was damaged by the Loma Prieta Earthquake of 1989, and eventually torn down. Soon afterwards, the part of the freeway, to the south of the station, between Third and Sixth Streets was also removed.

This station is a short walk to the San Francisco Giants' baseball stadium at 3rd & King. On game days Caltrain provides two special trains that leave 15 & 20 minutes after the game ends.

Muni provides Metro service on the 'N' & 'T' light rail lines at a pair of stations at 4th & King; on game days Muni also provides extra light rail service on the 'S' shuttles. Multiple Muni bus lines also serve the station. In the future, the E line, a Muni line that will use historic equipment, may also serve the station.

At Seventh Street, three long blocks west of the station, the tracks make a 90 degree turn south into the Bayshore Cutoff. Before 1908, the tracks headed west along the Oceanview route.

In 1972, the Mission Revival station at 3rd and Townsend was torn down, SP's tracks were cut back to behind 4th street, and a new functional station was built at 4th & Townsend (now referred to as 4th & King).

Left; Inside the station at Fourth and King, the concrete "waffle" roof of the 70's station can be clearly seen.

Below: Passengers board a Bombardier train on Platform 9, San Francisco's Fourth and King Station. Flood lights for the SF Giants baseball stadium can be seen above the train at the far left.

In 1998, Muni Metro (San Francisco's light rail system) was extended to 4th & King.

View of the Caltrain station from Muni's light-rail platform.

The Townsend Street entrance to the Caltrain Station. The Warm Planet bike shop and bicycle parking are in the background (2010).

The steel and glass structure, added in December, 1998, gives a light and airy feeling to what had been a dark and congested station.

View to the platforms

22nd Street
(originally 23th Street)

1149 22nd Street, San Francisco, CA 94107
Opened: December, 1908
Relocated in 1975
Mile Post 1.9 (3.1 km)

22nd Street Station is a dark and dreary station located below Interstate 280. It is one of the few non-accessible stations in the Caltrain system. It is situated between tunnels 1 and 2 of the Bayshore Cutoff.

The stop was originally located one block south at 23rd Street. When the interstate highway was built above it, the station was slightly relocated. Southern Pacific never bothered to have the station re-named. CalTrain renamed the stop in 1983.

Many passengers using this station are San Francisco residents who park near 22nd and make a reverse commute from the City to high-tech jobs in Silicon Valley. Parking is scarce and expensive at 4th & King, but relatively available here.

Left & below: The 22nd Street Station lies in the shadow of Interstate 280. The simple platforms on either side of the tracks are accessed by long flights of utilitarian staircases from an overpass at 22nd Street.

Left: Simple shelter & metal stairs on the South bound platform at 22nd Street.

Newcombe Avenue
(originally 14th Avenue)

Newcombe Avenue, San Francisco, CA 94124
Opened: December, 1908
Abandoned: April 1, 1954
Mile Post 3.1 (5.0 km)

Newcombe Avenue was a lightly used station, located between 23rd Street and Paul Street. In the early 20th century San Francisco had one set of numbered streets and two sets of numbered avenues. This caused enormous confusion, so the set of numbered avenues in the southeast portion of the city were re-named. Each avenue was given a new name starting with the corresponding letter of the alphabet, so 14th Avenue was given a name starting with N, the 14th letter of the alphabet. The 14th Avenue station was renamed "Newcombe Avenue" in April of 1947 and was abandoned on April 1, 1954.

Paul Avenue

Paul Avenue, San Francisco, CA 94124
Opened 1908
Abandoned: July, 2005

Located between tunnels 3 and 4, Paul Avenue was lightly used and non-handicap accessible. Muni provided more frequent, more direct, and less expensive service into downtown.

The stop was closed in 2005 in order to simplify scheduling after the introduction of the Baby Bullet service. An Oakdale station may replace it, when and if City College opens a campus nearby. The simple platforms and small metal shelter at this location have completely disappeared.

Left: A wide spot where a shelter once stood is the only evidence that the trains once stopped at Paul Avenue.

Bay Shore

400 Tunnel Avenue, San Francisco, CA 94134
Opened: 1907; Rebuilt/reopened: March 22, 2004
Mile Post 5.2 (8.3 km)

Above: Transparent elevator towers provide access to the footbridge across the tracks.

The original Bay Shore station, just north of the San Francisco-San Mateo County border, opened in 1907, following the construction of the Bayshore Cutoff. South of the station, the Bay had been filled, and shops for the Southern Pacific had been constructed. The area is now derelict; plans for its redevelopment were placed on hold, following the economic crash of 2008. Work finally began on the new development in 2014. In 2004 Bay Shore Station was relocated slightly south. No longer within San Francisco, it is now south of the San Francisco-San Mateo County border. It is in a section of 4-track right-of-way constructed for the Baby Bullet Trains. The center tracks are used for express, non-stopping trains that can pass local trains at this location. Passengers are not allowed to cross the tracks at this station, but must use the footbridge over the tracks. The bridge is handicap accessible, with elevators at either end.

A new footbridge provides the otherwise barren Bay Shore Station with its visual identity. Mount San Bruno and the town of Brisbane are in the distance.

Above: A view of an express train from the foot bridge. San Francisco, and tunnel #2, are in the background. Former railroad lands on either side of station await re-development.

Above: An express train is rushing though the Bay Shore Station.

Above: A view from inside the footbridge over the Bayshore Station.

Visitacion

Brisbane, CA
Opened: December, 1908, Relocated 1938
Abandoned: 1945
Mile Post 6.5/7.0 (10.5/11.3 km)

Visitation opened in 1908. The station building burned in 1938, after which the stop was relocated half a mile to the south. The stop was abandoned in 1945. Visitacion was built on the in-filled Visitacion bay. The bay received its name from the nearby Visitacion Valley. Visitacion Valley may have been named because of a vision that Franciscan friars saw of the Virgin Mary on a local rock formation, or it may have been named because the Spanish discovered the valley on the feast day of the Virgin of Guadalupe.

Above: Visitation Station.

From the collection of the San Bruno Public Library

Butler Road

Butler Road, South San Francisco, CA
Opened: December, 1908
Abandoned: 1984

Located near Oyster Point in South San Francisco, this was first station stop to be abandoned after the commute was taken over by CalTrain. This stop was originally opened to provide service for the workers of a nearby U.S. Steel plant. The plant closed in 1980, and the stop abandoned four years later.

South San Francisco

590 Dubuque Avenue, South San Francisco, CA 94080
Opened: 1909, remodeled & modernized 1942
Station building demolished: June, 1999
Mile Post 9.3 (15.0 km)

The City of South San Francisco was incorporated in 1908 when the towns of Baden and South San Francisco merged. At the time it was the major industrial center in San Mateo County with steel mills, meat packing plants, and other industries. South San Francisco sits on the southern slope of Mt. San Bruno. During the 1920's, the logo "South San Francisco, the Industrial City" was written on the side of Sign Hill, a hill on the southern slope of Mt. San Bruno. After WWII the heavy industries were replaced with light industries and high tech companies such as Genentech. The Station is officially named "South San Francisco," but Caltrain conductors usually refer to it as "South City".

Right: A small passenger station was built by SP in 1909 and modernized in 1942. The station was torn down June, 1999 and replaced with simple bus-stop like shelters.

Left: Waiting room and ticket counter at the former South San Francisco Southern Pacific Station.

Below: Only local trains stop at South San Francisco. The Grand Avenue overpass provides a little bit of protection to waiting passengers. South San Francisco is the only full-time station where (in 2015) passengers must cross the south-bound tracks to reach north-bound trains.

Right: Very little freight service remains on the Caltrain right-of-way between Santa Clara and San Francisco, But what does remain can usually be observed at South San Francisco.

Tanforan Loop

Opened: 1907
Closed 1970's

When the Bayshore cutoff opened in 1907, a loop connection was created between the new route and the old Oceanview route. A loop commute service was provide along the single track Oceanview route by running along the Bayshore route from the City in the mornings to Tanforan (in San Bruno) and then back to the City along the Oceanview route. In the Evenings this would be reversed, with commutes running out of the City over the Oceanview route and then back via the Bayshore.

The remains of the loop connection between the Bayshore and the Oceanview lines can still be seen in San Bruno near Tanforan were railroad tracks can be seen running into a crescent shaped open space between the streets of Bayshore Circle North and Bayshore Circle South.

Above: Bayshore Circle street sign

Left: Tracks, partly buried in asphalt, running into the crescent shaped open space.

Below: San Bruno BART station, on what had been Southern Pacific's Oceanview line, seen from where the loop from the Bayshore line met the original line.

San Bruno

The railroad has stopped in San Bruno since the 1860's, when the SF&SJ Rail Road was built. In early days, the San Bruno House, an inn, served as the railroad's station. In the late 19th century the ranches around San Bruno supplied San Francisco with meat and milk. After the Great San Francisco Earthquake of 1906, new neighborhoods developed around the station, and in 1914, San Bruno, with a population of 1,400, became an incorporated city. However most of the city's growth followed World War II.

The original station was located near the present Interstate 380. When the freeway was built, the San Bruno and Lomita Park stations were consolidated into one station at a point midway between the two.

From the collection of the San Bruno Public Library

Above: The wooden station building at San Bruno was built in 1916 and torn down in 1963.

Above: San Bruno lost its station when Interstate 380 was built. Between 1963 and 2014, simple bus-stop like structures provided shelter for waiting passengers at the stop located halfway between the former San Bruno and Lomita Park stations (2010).

The tracks at San Bruno were elevated to eliminate three seperate road level crossings. A new station was built on the elevated structure, shown during construction in August, 2012.

The new station at San Bruno opened April 1, 2014.

Above: A south bound train pulls into the new elevated station (May 2014)

Right: The new station is fully accessible with elevator tower for each platform; this is the tower for the north-bound platform.

Below: Two conductors prepare the train to depart from the north-bound platform over San Bruno Avenue, early morning in May 2014.

Above: A long sensuous ramp leads up to the platform from a new plaza along Huntington Avenue. A series of cascading waterfalls follows the ramp from platform level down to plaza level.

Lomita Park

Butler Road, South San Francisco, CA
Opened: 1911
Abandoned: 1963
Mile Post 12.1 (19.5 km)

Lomita was located just 1.1 miles south of the original San Bruno Station. A shelter was built at this location in 1911 to compete with the electric San Francisco and San Mateo Interurban Railroad. The lightly used stop was consolidated with the San Bruno stop in 1963 when freeway construction forced the relocation of San Bruno's main station.

From the collection of Jack Tillmany

A San Francisco Municipal Railroad Line 40 car passes the SP's Lomita Park Station in November, 1948, the Muni line would soon be abandoned.

Millbrae

(originally 17 Mile House)

100 California Drive, Millbrae, CA 94030
Opened: 1864 (BART/Caltrain Station: June, 2003)
Mile Post 13.7 (22.0 km)
(Old Depot) National Register #78000770

This station was originally called 17 Mile House (17 miles from San Francisco via the Oceanview route). In 1864, Millbrae received its present name from financier Darius Ogden Mills, an early land owner in the area who donated the land for the station. Mills also gave his name to Mills Field, the airport built in an unincorporated area to the east of Millbrae and San Bruno. Mills Field developed into today's San Francisco International Airport.

Millbrae remained rural until World War II; after the war it rapidly suburbanized. The city of Millbrae was incorporated in 1948.

In June 2003, the Bay Area Rapid Transit system (BART) was extended to Millbrae. At the same time, a new intermodal station, serving both the existing Caltrain and the newly extended BART, was opened. The Caltrain/BART station is the fourth Millbrae station. The first two station buildings burned, and the third station building is now a museum.

Right: An escalator from the Caltrain platform to the distribution concourse that is located over the Caltrain and BART tracks. Caltrain's southbound platform can be reached directly from California Drive. The northbound platform and the BART platforms can be accessed only from the distribution concourse.

Below: The two tracks serving Caltrain are on the west side of the station, (as is Millbrae's commercial center). Three tracks serving BART are to the east, (as is a large parking garage). Cross platform interchange is available between northbound Caltrain and BART.

Above: When the new BART/Caltrain intermodal station was built, the grade-level crossing at Millbrae Avenue was eliminated with an overpass above over the tracks.

Above: In 1864, soon after the San Francisco & San Jose Rail Road opened, Millbrae was served by an adobe depot. This first depot burned in 1890, and was replaced with a wooden structure. The second station burned in 1906. The third station (above) opened in 1907. The Colonial Revival building is painted in the classic Southern Pacific color scheme of SP Colonial Yellow and SP Dark Yellow. The station is a two story version of the "Harriman Standard" used by the railroads controlled by E.H. Harriman in the early 20th century (including the SP). The 74 by 46 foot building housed station agents on second floor until 1964.
In 1978, spurred on by Southern Pacific's threats to demolish the structure in order to increase parking at the station, the Millbrae Historical Society successfully placed the building on the National Register of Historic Places. Two years later, in August of 1980, the depot was moved to its present location, 21 East Millbrae Avenue (200 feet to the south of its former location) to accommodate the widening of Millbrae Avenue. Millbrae Avenue was later raised on an bridge over the Caltrain and BART tracks. The Millbrae station building was given to the city at the time of its move.
This structure continued to serve as the Caltrain depot until 2003 when the new Caltrain/BART intermodal station opened on the north side of Millbrae Avenue. Caltrain still uses the baggage room and offices on the second floor. The waiting room and ticket office now houses the Millbrae Train Museum. Check http://www.millbraehs.org/ for hours of operation.

Broadway Burlingame
(originally Buri Buri, Easton from 1917)

1190 California Drive,
Burlingame, CA 94010
Opened: 1911
Weekend only: July 2005

When Broadway's first station opened in 1911, it was a simple structure; it was supplemented with the present structure (now used as a restaurant) in 1928. Broadway Burlingame was originally called "Buri-Buri". The station was re-named "Easton" in honor of a nephew of Darius Ogden Mills (after which "Millbrae" had been named) who built a nearby housing estate. The station was finally re-named "Broadway Burlingame" in recognition of the street and town where it is located.

The San Francisco-San Mateo Electric Railway (which became part of the Market Street Railroad and eventually the San Francisco Municipal Railway's 40 line) stopped on the street side of the station until the line was abandoned in 1949.

Caltain still stops at the station on weekend, but not on weekdays. Present plans are to re-instate weekday service after electrification of the line. As in Atherton, College Park, and South San Francisco, passengers must cross the south-bound tracks to reach north-bound trains.

Right: A view of Broadway Burlingame, ca 1939. The original station was built with a pergola at each end. The northern pergola was eventually torn down, while the southern one was enclosed to connect with the 1926 station.

Below: Track-side view of the former station building.

From the collection of Jack Tillmany

Above: A view of the 1926 station, autumn, 2010. The area in front of the station has been landscaped.

Right: A view of the Station c. 1985. The original Buri Buri Station is the small gabled structure on the left. The 1926 Station is the tile roof structure on the right. The flat-roofed structure was originally an opened pergola that was in-filled during World War II.

Below: A view of the original station, summer 2010.

Burlingame

290 California Drive, Burlingame, CA 94010
Opened: October 10, 1894 ;
Platforms renovated February 25, 2008
Mile Post 16.3 (26.2 km)
National Register # 78000769, State Landmark No. 846

The Burlingame station was built in 1894 by the Southern Pacific Railroad and the Burlingame Country Club, the first country club on the West Coast. The Southern Pacific donated the cost of an ordinary station, and members of the country club, including many of San Francisco's financial elite, made up the difference in the cost of the station. This was the first permanent structure in California built in the Mission Revival style (also call "Spanish Revival" or "Moorish Revival"). Roof tiles were taken from two of California's Spanish built missions; Mission San Antonio de Padua (south of Monterey) and Mission Delores Asistencia in San Mateo.

Many of SP's stations built after 1894 were built in this style, including San Francisco's 1914 station at Third and Townsend, destroyed 1972 (see pg. 17), and the station at Gilroy (see pg. 86).

A waiting arcade, to the north of the station was added c. 1920.

The station was placed on the National Register of Historic Places in 1973, and restored in 1984-86, after it was purchased by the State of California.

A Market Street Railroad car passes in front of the Burlingame Station, ca. 1939.

From the collection of Jack Tillmany

Above: View of the station from the street side. The dirt road from the station to the country club developed into Burlingame Avenue. Burlingame's downtown district runs along the avenue from the station to El Camino Real, about a quarter mile to the west. El Camino Real (The King's Highway) dates back to the days when Spain ruled California. El Camino Real was the main highway between San Francisco and points south until after World War Two, when Highway 101 and Interstate 280 were built. Many of the town's along the Peninsula have downtown districts that stretch between their old Southern Pacific stations and El Camino Real.

Above is a view of Burlingame's distinctive arcade.

Above: An open arcade was added north of the original arcade around 1920.

Left: New shelters were built in 2008, when new platforms were constructed on the north-bound side of the rails.

Below: The arcade between the station and the tracks has been providing shelter for passengers since the 1890's.

Right: Historic landmark monument: "BURLINGAME RAILROAD STATION
This first permanent building in the Mission Revival style of architecture was designed by George H Howard and J.B. Mathison and financed by local residents and the Southern Pacific Railroad. It opened on October 10, 1894. The roof used 18th century tiles from the Mission San Antonio de Padua at Jolon and the Mission Dolores Asistencia at San Mateo."

Above: North-bound train with Bombardier's bi-level cars and a MPI locomotive in push mode. A wrought-iron fence was added between the tracks to prevent passengers from crossing the tracks at the station.

Left: A small park-like space next to the station.

Below: An example of the old Southern Pacific logo, with the rails heading into the sunset, can still be found at Burlingame.

San Mateo

385 First Avenue, San Mateo, CA 94401
Opened: October 17, 1863, relocated: Sept. 24, 2000
Mile Post 17.9 (28.8 km)

In 1793, a small wayside mission was founded on the banks of San Mateo Creek. Nothing remains of the mission structures, although some of the roof tiles were re-used on the Burlingame train station. In 1863 the San Francisco and San Jose Rail Road was built through San Mateo. San Mateo was one of the line's original stops, appearing in timetables from as early as 1863. Charles B. Polhemus, the director of railroad construction, chose the site for the stop, and soon businesses and residences followed. The first station, built in the 1870's, was of standard SF&SJRR design and was similar to the passenger section of the Santa Clara station. The original station was replaced by a second station in 1891, and a third station in 1925, designed by the architectural firm of Colby & Owsley.

In 1976, San Mateo's historic train station was torn down and replaced with a small ticket office in the ground floor of a two story parking structure. SP ticket agents were unhappy with the working conditions in the parking structure, complaining of the vibrations and smell of gasoline. The parking structure was torn down and replaced with a multiplex movie theatre at the same time that San Mateo's station was relocated two blocks to the north.

The present station was opened on September 24, 2000.

Right: The Mediterranean inspired 1925 station. This was San Mateo's third station building. The San Mateo station was the end of the line for Muni's 40 line, seen here (ca. 1940).

Below: This is the fifth station building in San Mateo, a vast improvement over the bunker-like fourth station. The present station houses a restaurant, a small police station, and the entrance to an underground parking structure.

From the collection of Jack Tillmany

Above: A covered area protects passengers waiting on the north-bound platform. In the center is an elevator and on either side are staircases that lead to underground parking and the south-bound platform.

Below: A view of the south-bound platform from across San Mateo Creek.

Above: Passengers wait to board a north-bound train.

Above: An express train ("Baby-Bullet") speeds through the San Mateo station.

Hayward Park

(Originally Leslie)

401 Concar Drive, San Mateo, CA 94401
Opened: late 1800's, relocated 1999
Mile Post 19.1 (30.7 km)

The Southern Pacific stop at Hayward Park was originally call Leslie. The original stop was at 16th Avenue, just east of "B" Street. The Hayward Park neighborhood received it's name from the estate of Alvinza Hayward, built in 1880. Hayward, who received his money from silver mining and from banking, was said to be California's first millionaire. The estate, after being converted into a hotel, burned down in the 1920's after which the area was redeveloped as a suburban housing estate. In 1936, the name of the stop was changed from Leslie to Hayward Park.

The historic Hayward Park neighborhood is to the west of the railroad tracks. Until 1999, the original SP station was centered in the neighborhood next to a small park called Hayward Square. In 1999, the station was moved about a half mile south, next to Highway 92, and parking was added. A new transit oriented development, to be named "Hayward Park Green," is proposed east of the station.

Above: The new Hayward Park Station with easy access to Highway 92

Above: Hayward Square, a small park across from the former Hayward Park stop

Bay Meadows

San Mateo, CA 94403
Opened: 1901
Abandoned: December 2005
Mile Post 19.9 (32.7 km)

Bay Meadows, a horse-racing track, was located just to the northeast of the Hillsdale station. Before December 2005, there had been a station located at Bay Meadow less than 1/2 mile (800m) north of Hillsdale. Many trains stopped here during the racing season. In 2008, the Bay Meadows racetrack closed and was torn down. A large transit oriented development with 1,171 residential units, 93,000 sq. ft. of retail and 715,000 sq. ft. of office space is to be built on the site of the closed racetrack and support structures. Work on the project began in 2008, but when the housing market collapsed the project went into hiatus. In 2013, construction on the project has resumed.

Hillsdale
(Originally Beresford)

3333 El Camino Real, San Mateo, CA 94403
Opened: 1901, relocated 2005
Mile Post 20.3 (32.7 km)

The first station at Hillsdale (named Beresford) was opened in 1901. In 1942, it was replaced with the present structure, a colonial revival building. The Colonial revival building was donated to the Southern Pacific by local land developers. At the same time that the new building opened, the station was renamed Hillsdale.

In 1965, when SP raised the tracks onto a bridge across Hillsdale Blvd (see photo below), the tracks were also moved slightly to the east, and lifted onto an embankment, the station building now sits below platform level.

When Hillsdale's platforms were rebuilt in 2005, they were extended several hundred feet north and the Bay Meadows station was closed (see above). It has been proposed that the Hillsdale station be moved north from 31st Street to 28th Street to better serve Bay Meadow's redevelopment. This would bring the station close to where the abandoned Bay Meadows station had been.

Right: The platforms on the bridge over Hillsdale Avenue were abandoned when the station was relocated slightly to the north in 2005.

Below, In 2010, Luke's Local, a small coffee house, occupied the 1942 station building. As of March 2015 the station building is occupied by "Javaddictions".

A shelter, built at the time of Hillsdale Boulevard's grade separation in 1965, still survives on Hillsdale south bound platform; its twin on the north-bound platform disappeared years ago.

In the summer of 2010, a south-bound train stops at Hillsdale.

Above is a typical handicap accessible ramp for use with Bombardier cars. Gallery cars must use mechanical lifts (see pg.12).

Belmont

995 El Camino Real, Belmont, CA 94002
Opened: September 1863
Elevated Station Opened: June 8, 2000
Mile Post 21.9 (35.2 km)

Belmont, California is located in the Cañada Diablo, a small valley in the Coast Range.

Belmont was served by the first trains to run on the San Francisco and San Jose Rail Road in 1863. The president of the SF&SJ, Henry Mayo Newhall, was a resident of Belmont. Although trains stopped at Belmont from the beginning of operations, it wasn't until 1867 that Belmont received a depot of its own, and even that was a second hand building (similar to the passenger part of the Santa Clara depot) hauled up from Menlo Park after a new station had been built there. The second-hand station burned in 1872 and was replaced in February 1873. Belmont was incorporated in 1926.

One and a half miles of embankment were constructed though the towns of Belmont and San Carlos in the late 1990's. Grade crossings though the two towns were eliminated when the elevated line opened on June 8, 2000.

Left & Below: The present station opened when the tracks through Belmont were moved onto an embankment in June of 2000 and level crossings in the towns of Belmont and San Carlos were eliminated.

Above & Below: Belmont is one of the few Caltrain stations with center platforms. The platform are reached by stairs, or via an elevator in the clock tower.

Above: A south-bound train is about to depart Belmont.

San Carlos

599 El Camino Real, San Carlos, CA 94070
Opened: 1888
Elevated Station Opened: June 8, 2000
Mile Post 23.2 (37.3 km)
National Register # 74000556

Some historians believe that on November 4, 1769, (the feast day of Saint Charles) the explorer Gaspar de Portola first sighted the San Francisco Bay from the hills that now lie in San Carlos. Developers in the mid 19th century named the area San Carlos in reference to this belief.

San Carlos was the first suburb built on the Peninsula. The San Carlos Land & Improvement Company, owned in part by SP's officials, was organized in 1887 to promote residential development (but not industrial or commercial activity) in the area. The San Carlos is rare example of a California railroad station in the Richardsonian Romanesque style, though the style was common for railroad stations in the East. SP and the land company built the station in 1888, but the station remained too large for the small surrounding population and at times parts of the station were leased out for use as a post office, a library and a house of worship. By 1925, with a population of 600, the area had grown large enough to incorporate, although the surrounding area remained rural until after World War II, after which it quickly filled with homes. San Carlos now has a population of 27,238 people.

The station's ticket office closed in 1967, and again the building was leased out, first as a real estate office, and since 1984, as the Depot Cafe. The station was bought by the state in 1982 (the first station bought by the state) and renovated in 1985.

Above: A view of the station from across the tracks in 1989, before the tracks were moved onto an embankment.

Right: The Southern Pacific Railroad built the Richardsonian Romanesque Revival station in San Carlos in 1888. It is similar in style and material to buildings on the Stanford University campus and may have been designed by Charles Coolidge, the architect responsible for that campus. The university had been founded by Leland Stanford, the president of the Southern Pacific Railroad. In 1976 the station building became a city landmark, and in 1984 was put on the National Register of Historical Places.

Above: The original station, as seen from El Camino Real.

The San Carlos platforms are on a raised embankment built during the 1990's.

During 1990's, grade level crossings were eliminated in the towns of San Carlos and Belmont. The Caltrain tracks were raised onto an embankment, with pedestrian and automobile traffic crossing below the tracks. At the San Carlos Station a pedestrian underpass leads from the original station to the northbound platforms

Redwood City

One James Avenue, Redwood City, CA 94063
Opened: 1863
Redwood City Transit Center dedicated July 13, 1995
Mile Post 25.4 (40.9 km)

Redwood City owes it founding to the existence of a deep water channel that leads from the Bay's open water, through mud flats of the South Bay, to the present site of downtown Redwood City. A wharf was established where lumber, mostly redwood from the Santa Cruz mountains, was shipped to San Francisco. The town was originally called Mezesville, after the local land owner who drew up the original plan for the town. However the locals preferred the name Redwood, and when a post office was established in 1856, it was called Redwood City. That was also the year that Redwood City became the county seat of San Mateo County, a new county carved from the southern part of San Francisco County. The Port of Redwood City is still the Bay's only deep water port south of San Francisco.

After the railroad arrived in 1863, the town's population boomed, and in 1868, the city became the first incorporated town in San Mateo County. Many wealthy San Franciscans built country estates in the area.

The next boom came after the earthquake of 1906 when the large estates were subdivided and sold. After World War II, as in much of the Peninsula, the population exploded.

The original train station in Redwood City (built in the 1870's) was replaced with a larger stucco and wood building in 1909. The 1909 station was the only station north of San Jose that was built on the east side of the tracks. In 1937 the station was moved to the west side. The second station burned in 1979; for many years after that a portable structure was used as a ticket office. The present waiting structure was opened in 1995.

Redwood City may be a station on the California High Speed Rail.

Redwood City's motto is "Climate Best By Government Test." Before World War One, the US and German governments conducted a climate survey and declared that the Canary Islands, off North Africa's coast, and the area centered on Redwood City, to have the world's best climate.

On July 13, 1995, the present Redwood City Transit Center was dedicated.

A south-bound train is arriving in Redwood City, Summer 2010.

A shopping center, named "Sequoia Station" faces onto Redwood City's south-bound platforms.

A commuter train, in push mode, is about to depart from Redwood City on a mild day in the Summer of 2010.

Redwood Junction

A mile south of Redwood City is the junction for the Dumbarton line. When the line is finally rebuilt for commute service, half of the trains from Union City will head north to San Francisco, and half will head south for Silicon Valley and San Jose.

Atherton

(originally Fair Oaks)

1 Dinkelspiel Station Lane, Atherton, CA 94027
Opened: 1866 (Weekends only from July 2005)
Milepost: 27.8 (44.7 km)

A flag stop was established at the community of Fair Oaks (which later became Atherton) in 1866. Fair Oaks was the location of several large estates in what was then the northern part of the unincorporated town of Menlo Park. In 1923, Menlo Park considered municipal incorporation and attempted to include Fair Oaks. However, Fair Oaks, wishing to maintain its exclusivity, and to prevent commercial operation in its area, hurriedly incorporated on its own. A town within California already had the name of Fair Oaks, so the community chose to use the name Atherton, after an early land owner in the area. A small amount of commercialization has occurred along El Camino Real, but the rest of the community has remained residential, with minimum lot sizes of one acre.

The Tuscan columned station at Atherton was restored in 1990. The station was repainted in its original colors and the original benches refinished. Old-style lampposts and stone gateway pillars on Fair Oaks drive were also added.

Atherton remained a local stop until 2005, when, because of its low use, it became (along with Broadway Burlingame) a weekend-only stop. However, there are plans to re-instate weekday service after Caltrain is electrified.

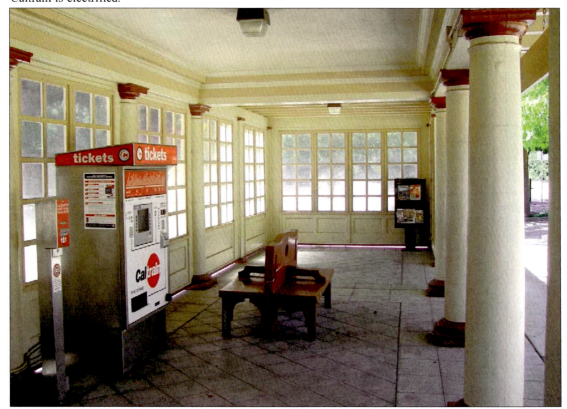

Above: A beautifully restored, but lightly used shelter.

Above: A north-bound train passes through Atherton

The well-maintained Atherton stop preserves a classic suburban ambiance.

Atherton's tile-roofed railway station was built in 1913 and the flat-roofed wings, sympathetic to the original, were added in 1954. The whole building was restored in 1990, and, although little used, is in excellent condition.

Menlo Park

(originally Big Trees)

1120 Merrill Street, Menlo Park, CA 94025
Opened: 1863, Present station from 1867
Mile Post 28.9 (46.5 km)
National Register # 74000556, State Landmark No. 955

Menlo Park was originally called "Big Trees Station" "Big Trees" is the English translation of Palo Alto. The station was named for the large redwood trees around San Franciscito Creek.

A pair of brothers-in-law, from Menlough, County Galway in Ireland, bought property in the area in 1854. They built homes next to each other, and above the common drive leading to the two houses they erected a tall arch with the name "Menlo Park". Railroad officials adopted the name for the local stop. In 1874 Menlo Park (including what is now Atherton and East Palo Alto) became the second incorporated city within San Mateo County, but Menlo Park disincorporated two years later. In 1927, Menlo Park again incorporated, this time without Atherton or East Palo Alto.

Menlo Park is one of two surviving stations built by the San Francisco and San Jose Rail Road (the other is Santa Clara). It served as the main stop for nearby Stanford University until Palo Alto was built. Victorian trim was added during the 1890's and a north-side shelter was built during World War One to serve the military at nearby camp Fremont. The Menlo Park Chamber of Commerce has occupied the station building since the 1960's, on July 4, 1983, the Menlo Park Station became a California historical Landmark.

Right: The station building at Menlo Park was built in 1867. The original station, from 1863, was shipped to Belmont in 1867, and burned in 1872. A historic marker at the front of the station claims it to be the oldest passenger station in California, but this is not true. The confusion may have arisen because the oldest station, Santa Clara, was moved from its original location on the east side of the tracks to the west side. So Menlo Park is the oldest passenger station on its original site, but not the oldest station.

Postcard from the author's collection

The number of people using the station increased during World War One after the army opened the nearby Camp Fremont (now the Veterans Hospital); so in 1917, the waiting room was expanded 14 feet and a 40-foot open air shelter was added to the north side of the station.

In 1987, the California Department of Transportation (Caltrans) bought and rehabilitated the depot and baggage house, and added a bicycle storage structure and a clock tower. Caltrans also added an off-street bus station and new commuter parking. On June 27, 1987, the "Menlo Park Transportation Center was dedicated.

A baggage building was added to the station to serve Camp Fremont in 1917; later the baggage room was used by Railway Express until 1928. It was moved to its present location in 1986. The building has been partially occupied by The West Bay Model Railroad Association since 1948; the part not occupied by the WBRA contains bicycle storage. See wbmrra.ning.com for hours that the building is open to the public.

Above: The 1987 enclosed bicycle storage structure.

Palo Alto

95 University Avenue, Palo Alto, CA 94301
Opened: November 1893, Present station from 1941
Mile Post 30.1 (48.4 km)
National Register # 1996000425

Palo Alto received its name from a pair of tall redwood trees mentioned by the Spanish missionary Francisco Palou in 1774, one of the ancient trees still survives near San Franciscito Creek.

Leland Stanford, one of the Big Four of the Southern Pacific, and the president of the railroad, bought a 650 acre ranch near Palo Alto in 1876. Stanford's son, Leland Stanford Jr. died in 1884 at the age of 15; soon afterwards, Leland Stanford founded the Leland Stanford Jr. University, in memory of his son, on the grounds of his ranch.

The university was served by Menlo Park until Palo Alto's first station was built in 1893 (and replaced with a larger station in 1897). Stanford University is to the west of the station, and downtown Palo Alto is to the east.

By the 1940's a grade separation project at University Avenue in Palo Alto necessitated the relocation of the station. Construction on Palo Alto's railroad station begun in 1940 and the art deco, streamline moderne station opened on March 8, 1941. The concrete and stucco building is enhanced with aluminum, stainless steel and glass block accents.

Until 1971, the building also served long distance trains such as the Lark, the Coast Daylighter and the Del Monte. In the future, it is a possible location for a mid peninsula stop for the California High Speed Rail.

Both the Palo Alto transit center (for buses) and the main building, west of the tracks, are on land leased from Stanford University, the tracks and the shelter on the east side are owned by Caltrain.

The ticket office was closed in the early 21st century after Caltrain adopted the proof-of-payment system. The interior now houses a cafe.

This example of streamline modern architecture has all the features associated with the style inspired by modern machinery: glass block, horizontal lines and porthole windows. This station was seen to complement the streamline trains, such as the Coast Daylighter, that were gaining popularity at the time it was built.

A Pedestrian passes below the tracks at Palo Alto

Streamline shelter on the north-bound platform complements the main station.

San Francisco-bound train about to depart Palo Alto, summer 2010.

Southern Pacific logo above the entrance to the Caffe del Doge.

The waiting room and mural were designed by John McQuarrie. The mural's themes are of transportation and the establishment of Stanford University.

Stanford
(originally Stadium)

100 Embarcadero Road., Palo Alto, CA 94301
Opened: early 20th century
refurbish 1985

The Stanford Station, located near the Stanford University Stadium, is only open on game days, or other special events when designated trains serve the station. This simple stop sees large crowds when the "Big Game Specials", a century old tradition, run.

The platforms at Stanford were refurbished for Superbowl XIX in which the local favorites, the San Francisco 49ers, defeated the Miami Dolphins on January 20, 1985.

There are no ticket machines located at this station. Passengers without passes are advised to purchase return tickets at their originating station before boarding the train to Stanford.

Above: Passengers cross the tracks after a train pulls out of Stanford.

Right: Passengers board a train after a home game at Stanford, October 6, 2012.

Below: The Stanford stop is gated and locked at most times; open only on game days or during other special events. The Stanford stop only has simple concrete platforms, sufficient for its limited use.

California Avenue

(originally Mayfield)

101 California Avenue Palo Alto, CA 94306
Opened: October 1863
Present station opened: 1983
Mile Post 31.8 (51.2 km)

California Avenue, originally known as Mayfield, served as the southern most station of the San Francisco & San Jose Rail Road when it opened in October 1863; the line was extended to San Jose in January 1864.

Mayfield Farm was given its name in 1854, and soon after the railroad established a stop at this location, where a small unincorporated town, also called Mayfield, developed. The first station building was built in 1891. In 1940 Mayfield was annexed by Palo Alto, and the name of its station was changed to California Avenue.

The original station was replaced with a simple station house in 1954, and that, in turn, was replaced with the present mission-style building in 1983. In 2008, a pedestrian underpass was excavated beneath the tracks. North-bound passengers no longer cross the tracks at grade, and Caltrain's schedule isn't disrupted when trains pass at the station.

For many years commute trains ran from San Francisco to Los Gatos via a line that branched out from the Peninsula line just south of California Avenue. The line was abandoned in 1964 and its right-of-way was used for the Foothill Expressway.

Right: Now closed ticket office, replaced by automated ticket machines and the "Clipper Card" readers seen to either side of the old ticket window

Above: The station house was built in 1983, soon after CalTrain gained control of the system.

Left: The north-bound platform opened in 2008.

San Antonio

(originally Castro, later Rengstorff)

190 Showers Drive, Mountain View, CA 94040
(the Castro stop opened: 1863, Closed Feb. 6, 2000)
San Antonio open: April, 1999
Mile Post 34.1 (54.9 km)

In 1851, Mariano Castro and family built their first home near what later became the Corner of Rengstorff Ave. & Central Blvd. In 1860, the family donated land to the San Francisco and San Jose Rail Road for Mountain View's first flag stop. The stop was named 'Castro'; the area surrounding the stop became known as Castroville.

The name 'Castro' caused confusion, as the station in downtown Mountain View was on a street also named Castro, so the stop called 'Castro' wasn't on Castro Street, and the stop on Castro Street wasn't called Castro. After CalTrain assumed control of the route, 'Castro' was renamed 'Rengstorff'.

The stop at Rengstorff Avenue in Mountain View (mile post 34.9) was closed in 2000, several months after a new station opened 8/10ths of a mile to the northwest at San Antonio Boulevard.

The simple shelter at the former Castro/Rengstorff stop,

Mountain View Historical Society

A colorful portal leads to the pedestrian underpass below the tracks.

A San Jose bound train is pulling into the station. San Antonio Boulevard crosses over the track on the overpass in the background.

Mountain View
600 West Evelyn Avenue, Mountain View, CA 94041
Opened: 1888
Mile Post 36.1 (58.1 km)

In 1842, The Mexican government granted the Rancho Pastoria de las Borregas to Francisco Esrada and his wife Inez Castro. The northern portion of the rancho was sold to Inez's brother Mariano Castro who later sold part of his property to S.O. Houghton. When The San Francisco and San Jose Rail Road built the line through the area, Houghton donated part of his property, near Castro Street and Evelyn Avenue, for a train stop. The new station shifted the focus of the young community of Mountain View from the original settlement near El Camino and Grand Road to what we know now as Downtown Mountain View.

By the time of its incorporation on November 7, 1902, there were 611 residents living in downtown Mountain View.

Mountain View is at the center of the high-tech Silicon Valley and is the third busiest station in the system, after San Francisco (Fourth and King) and Palo Alto.

Above: A train of Sumitomo gallery cars and a train of Bombardier bi-levels meet at Mountain View. To the right is a ramp used for wheelchair access to the Bombardier cars. A steel plate bridges the gap between the platform and the car's floor. The gallery cars use an internal, mechanical lift for wheelchair access.

Left: A view of the 1888 station from across the tracks. This station was at Front Street (now Evelyn Avenue) opposite View Street. It was several hundred feet south of where the replica station (next page) was built.

The original station was built in 1888 and torn down by the Southern Pacific in 1959. It was replaced with a concrete shelter which was later removed by Caltrain.

The replica station building at Mountain View, used as a cafe and bicycle storage, was built in 2001. The building was based on a standard Southern Pacific style (SP#18) in use in 1888, the year that Mountain View's original station opened. The exterior of the building is similar to the original station destroyed in 1959, although the interior is not.

In 1999, VTA extended its light rail system to the Mountain View station

Sunnyvale
(originally Murphy Station)

121 W. Evelyn Avenue, Sunnyvale, CA 94086
Opened: 1863
Rebuilt: May 2003
Mile Post 38.8 (62.4 km)

In 1842, the Mexican government granted the Rancho Pastoria de las Borregas to Francisco Estrada. In 1850, Estrada sold the southern portion to Martin Murphy Jr. for $12,500. Murphy established a wheat farm and ranch named Bay View.

In 1860, The San Francisco and San Jose Rail Road was allowed to lay tracks through the Bay View Ranch and established Murphy Station. Murphy's ranch became the nucleus of the city of Sunnyvale.

The original station, built in 1896, was heavily damaged by a tornado in 1952 and replaced with a simple modern structure, and in turn, that building was replaced by the present station in 2003.

Between 1950 and 1970 the population of Sunnyvale increased 1000% and has increased another 150% in the years since 1970.

A farmer's market is held in the surface parking lot at the Sunnyvale station every Saturday.

Right: Original station.

Below: The rebuilt $11,400,000 Sunnyvale Transit Center opened in 2003 included a new 400 space garage with a net increase of 217 new parking spaces.

Sunnyvale Public Library

Above: The elevator shaft for Sunnyvale's parking structure doubles as a modern clock tower.

Left: Ticket machines are located next to the parking structure.

Below: A San Francisco bound train leaves Sunnyvale.

Lawrence

137 San Zeno Way, Sunnyvale 94086
Opened: late 1800's, abandoned 1942,
Reopened: 1982, Rebuilt: March 2004
Mile Post 40.8 (65.6 km)

A stop at Lawrence was established on the southern edge of Martin Murphy Jr's Bay View Ranch in the late 1800's. The lightly used stop was abandoned by the Southern Pacific in 1942, leaving a gap of 5-1/2 miles between the stations at Sunnyvale and Santa Clara. While this area remained agricultural, this gap didn't matter. However, by the time CalTrain had taken over the commute, the area had begun to develop into part the of high tech industrial area now known as Silicon Valley. In 1982, CalTrain re-established the Lawrence stop with simple bus stop-like shelters. Lawrence was the first new (or re-established) station opened by the public authority. The station was re-built in its present form in 2004.

California Room, San Jose Public Library

Left: Lawrence Station in the early 20th Century consisted of a small ticket office/freight facility. Note the bicycle parking, a faint foreshadowing of what was to come. Caltrain now has one of the most enlightened bicycle policies of any commuter rail system in North America.

Below: An extra pair of tracks was added at Lawrence in the early 21st century to allow Baby Bullets to pass locals and limiteds. Trains stop at Lawrence only on the two outer tracks.

Left: A south-bound train unloads passengers on a sunny summer day in 2010. An underpass to the north-bound platform can be seen on the lower right of the photograph.
Note the bicyclists exiting the bicycle car.

Above & below: Wood and stone shelters were added to Lawrence when an extra pair of tracks for passing Baby Bullets was built in 2004. In the background of the photograph below, the Lawrence Expressway, passes over the tracks.

Santa Clara

1001 Railroad Avenue, Santa Clara, CA 95050
Opened: January 16, 1864
Mile Post 44.7 (71.9 km)
National Register # 1985000359

The Southern Pacific mainline (now Union Pacific), joins the Peninsula line just north of the Santa Clara station. Today's mainline (built in the 1870's) was formerly the narrow gauge South Pacific Coast Railroad that ran from Alameda to Santa Cruz. Amtrak's Coast Starlight and Capitol Corridor, along with Altamont Commuter Express (ACE) from Stockton, join Caltrain at this point.

The Caltrain station at Santa Clara is the oldest passenger train station in California. It was built at the same time as the pioneering San Francisco & San Jose Rail Road, and was one of two original-way stations between the cities.

The nearby University of Santa Clara was a significant backer of the railway. The passenger depot was originally located on the north side of the tracks. The Peninsula route, which leaves San Francisco heading south, swings in a wide arc so that when approaching Santa Clara the route is heading east; beyond San Jose, it will once more head south. The station building was moved to the south side of the tracks and attached to an existing freight house in 1877. Orchards followed the arrival of the railroad, and the area quickly became the center of a large fruit canning industry.

The station now houses the Edward Peterman Museum of Railroad History. The museum is operated by the South Bay Historical Railroad Society (check out sbhrs.org for more information). Inside are a railroad library, original artifacts from the station, and model railroads layouts. The station and museum is open to the public on Tuesdays and Saturdays.

Amtrak's Capitol Corridor & ACE (Altamont Corridor Express) also stop at this station. The acronym "ACE" originally stood for Altamont Commuter Express, but "Commuter" has recently been changed to "Corridor". There are plans to extend BART to Santa Clara, and if that happens, a people mover might be built to connect the station to the nearby Norman Y. Mineta San Jose International Airport. At present, a free bus shuttle is provided to the airport.

The Santa Clara Station is the oldest continuously operated train station in California. Everything this side of the bay window is part of the original station, built in the SF&SJRR's standard station design. By 1877 the passenger depot had been attached to the freight house, and by 1885 a further addition had brought it to its present size and shape (see pg. 2).

Santa Clara's tower, opened in 1926 and closed in 2009, is now part of the station's museum.

Passengers disembark from a south-bound train In the summer of 2010.

Outside the museum, a Pullman rail car from 1912 is being restored.

Above: In the summer of 2010, passengers still were required to cross the tracks at Santa Clara to access the north-bound trains.

Right: The pedestrian underpass to new island platform, both of which opened in February 2012

Below: Amtrak's "Capitol Corridor" train is stopped at platform "2". Island platforms "2" & "3" are used by north-bound Caltrain, ACE (Altamont Corridor Express) trains, and Amtrak's "Capitol Corridor". South-bound Caltrain uses platform "1", next to the station building.

College Park

Only two trains stop here in the morning (one in each direction) and two in the evening (again, one in each direction), for students of the Bellarmine College Prep.

The University of the Pacific (initially named California Wesleyan College) was founded by Methodist ministers in 1851. It was California's first chartered institution of higher learning. In 1871, The University of the Pacific moved from Santa Clara to San Jose. The area near its campus soon became known as College Park. In 1924 the University moved to Stockton and sold its San Jose Campus to the Catholic Society of Jesus. In the early 1920's, the Jesuit-run Santa Clara College, a school for secondary and college age students, separated into two schools, Santa Clara University and Santa Clara Prep. In 1925, Santa Clara Prep moved to the former University of the Pacific campus in College Park. After the move, the school changed its name to Bellarmine College Preparatory. College Park was the site of an early SP freight yard.

This station was immortalized by Jack London in the opening of "Call of the Wild" where the dog Buck is placed on a train and begins his journey to Alaska. The station at the time (1897) was just a flag stop.

Above is the shelter at College Park where students wait for their trains.

Students and other passengers must cross the tracks to access north bound trains. This is a lightly used station and there are no plans to build new platforms.

Caltrain Centralized Equipment Maintenance and Operational Facility

585 Lenzen Ave, San Jose, CA 95110
22 acres (8.9 ha)
Opened: September 29, 2007
(Completed 2008)

The new Caltrain Centralized Equipment Maintenance and Operational Facility was built on the site of the old Southern Pacific maintenance yard, just to the south of College Park. Caltrain's CEMOF consolidates operations formerly performed at various locations throughout the system. Included in the CEMOF are shops, a central control building (where dispatchers direct and manage train traffic on the system from San Francisco down to Gilroy), a train-washing facility, a fueling station, a water treatment plant, and a service and inspection area. Inside the maintenance shop are two 800 ft long service and inspection pits and a crane that can lift 25,000 pounds. Also included in the CEMOF is a tunnel to allow the three shifts of workers, who keep the facility active 24 hours-a-day, to pass safely under the active tracks.

"LITTLEWAGON", Caltrain's little red switcher.

The two photos above show the 58,000 square feet, three-story maintenance shop.

San Jose Diridon

65 Cahill Street, San Jose, CA 95110
Opened: December 30, 1935
Mile Post 47.5 (76.4 km)
Architect: John H. Christie
National Register # 1993000274

The first station in San Jose was located at San Pedro Street near St. James Park and was later moved to Market and Bassett Streets. The original line went though the center of San Jose's downtown. From College Park, the line turned east on Julian Street to a wood-framed station at Market Street. After passing the Market Street station, the line turned south and ran for fifteen blocks in the middle of Fourth Street.

By 1920, with the increase in both passenger and freight traffic, and with increasing conflicts with the newly popular automobile, the congestion on Fourth street had become intolerable. Southern Pacific's franchise on Fourth Street had expired in 1919, and the city was anxious for the removal of SP's tracks. Therefore, Southern Pacific developed plans to reconfigure its San Jose facilities.

The freight yard at College Park had been outgrown; so, a new freight yard was to be constructed at Santa Clara (it opened in 1927). A new double-tracked line was built, along with a modern passenger station, in an old industrial area on Cahill Street at the western edge of downtown. This is the largest station on the Caltrain line.

The Coast Line was also to be double-tracked from where the new line reconnected with the existing line to Logan. The double-tracking had reached as far as Gilroy by 1930, but then repercussions from the Great Depression put the project on hold, eventually to be canceled altogether. The depression also slowed the progress of the new line west of San Jose's city center. However, the necessity of removing trains from San Jose's streets kept the project alive.

The "San Jose Line Change" project was finally completed at the end of 1935. The new line followed the old Santa Cruz branch line (the old South Pacific Coast Railroad) along Los Gatos Creek. At Cahill Street, the site of the old South Pacific Coast Depot, an imposing Italian Renaissance Revival station was built. South of the station, a completely new six mile long grade-separated line was constructed. The new line reconnected with the old line at Lick Street. The tracks along Fourth Street were abandoned from Julian Street in the north to Valbrick Street in the south. South of Valbrick Street the old line was retained to service the industry in the area.

The station is 390 feet long and 78 feet wide (40' wide at the wings). The ceiling of the central waiting room rises three stories. Offices are on the upper floors of the two wings. A mural over the ticket

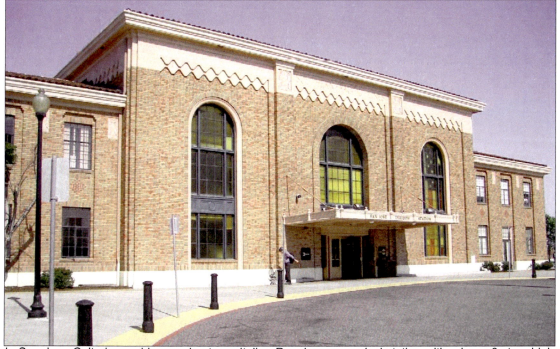

In San Jose Caltrain provides service to an Italian Renaissance revival station with a large 3-story high waiting room flanked by 2-story wings containing offices and support facilities.

counter highlights the transportation history of the Santa Clara Valley and the city of San Jose (the Coast Daylighter is prominently located in the mural). The station includes five tracks. The eastern most track is accessible from the station and is usually used by Amtrak. The other four tracks are accessible from two island platforms, reached via a pedestrian subway. Plans call for a California high-speed rail station, as well as a new BART station, to be located at this site.

At the end of the 20th century, the San Jose Station was rehabilitated and its parking was increased to 880 spaces. On December 8, 1994, the station was renamed "San Jose-Diridon Station" in honor of county supervisor Rod Diridon, a strong supporter of public transit and one of the moving forces behind the creation of Caltrain. At about the same time, Amtrak built a new maintenance facility south of the station.

The VTA light rail line runs through a new tunnel below the station, with a light rail station to the west of the tracks. The light rail station is reached via an extension of the existing pedestrian subway below the platforms. From this station the light rail follows the old South Pacific Coast Railroad route to Campbell.

San Jose sees 96 Caltrain trains per day (down from 98 in 2008). San Jose also sees two Coast Starlights per day, 14 Capitol Corridor trains, and 8 ACE trains (Altamont Corridor Express).

Above: The station at San Jose opened on December 31, 1935. The stations' exterior is brick with a terra cotta trim; the colors have been described as red & sunset, in reference to the Sunset Limited, which stopped at the station at that time (and would continue to be a stop on the Sunset Limited's route until World War II). This station was featured in the Alfred Hitchcock movie "Marnie"; where it stood-in for a Hardford, CT.station.

Photo by Terry Wade

Above: Waiting room, restrooms and a concession stand are located beyond the arch in the background. Doors on the right lead to the concourse seen on page 77.

Waiting room. The ticket counter is for Amtrak use only. Caltrain passengers must buy their tickets from a machine; Caltrain passengers may also use the "Clipper" card, the regional transit smart card.

The pedestrian underpass below the tracks. Passage to the VTA light rail is in the background.

A bicyclist walks up the ramp from the pedestrian underpass.

Caltrain, pulled by locomotive 916, waits at the platform.

Passengers waiting for Amtrak's Coast Starlight are in the concourse behind the main waiting room.

A neon news stand sign in the main waiting room.

The south-bound Coast Starlight pulls into San Jose-Diridon station, Summer 2010.

Gilroy Extension

The Peninsula Corridor Joint Powers Board consists of representatives from the counties of San Francisco, San Mateo, and Santa Clara. The board runs Caltrain and bought the 51.4 mile right-of-way from San Francisco to San Jose in 1991, as well as trackage rights between San Jose and Gilroy. On June 27, 1992 Caltrain extended its service to Gilroy.

Tamien

1355 Lick Avenue, San Jose, CA 95110
Opened: June 27, 1992
Mile Post 49.1 (79.0 km)

In 1992 a new station was built south of the Cahill Street station at West Alma Avenue. There are 400 parking spaces at Tamien. The new station is shared with the VTA light rail system. When the station opened, it was the first convenient transfer point between the two systems. At present (2015) convenient transfer points also exist at San Jose Diridon (pg. 73-77) and Mountain View (pg. 62 & 63). While both those stations connect to the Mountain View-Winchester line, only Tamien connects Caltrain to the VTA's Alum Rock-Santa Teresa line.

Tamien Station was originally to be called Alma (after the nearby avenue), but before the station opened the name was changed to honor the local Native Americans. Tamien was the Ohlone (local Native American) name for the area along the Guadalupe River that later became San Jose. The name was later extended to refer to the dialect of the Ohlone language spoken by the natives of the Santa Clara Valley.

Tamien station consists of two sets of island platforms. One set of platforms, to the east side of the limited access Highway 87, is used by Caltrain; and the other, in the median of Highway 87, is used by VTA light rail. The platforms are reached via an underpass below the railroad and highway.

The station is served by Caltrain only on weekdays; on weekends a shuttle bus runs between Tamien and Diridon Station.

Although the Tamien station was completed by March of 1992, SP refused to run trains to it, and the opening had to wait until after Amtrak began operating the trains in June 1992.

A Sumitomo train waits above the entrance to the Tamien Station.

Two trains wait at the island platforms for return runs to San Francisco.

A stairway and the only escalator on the system lead down to the passageway below

Embankment at Tamien.

Capitol

3400 Monterey Hwy., San Jose 95111
Opened: June 27, 1992
Mile Post 52.4 (84.3 km)

After the Loma Prieta earthquake of October 17, 1989, one daily Caltrain round trip was extended to Salinas from October 23, 1989, to November 10, 1989. Although the time-span of the operation was short, it emphasized the demand for increased commuter service south of San Jose.

Simple shelters and a platform are all that are required at this lightly used station.

View south from the station platform towards Century Theatres' Capitol Complex of drive-in theatres. Flea markets are held at the theatres on weekends, although the trains only run to the Capitol station on weekdays.

Blossom Hill

5560 Monterey Hwy., San Jose 95138
Opened: June 27, 1992
Mile Post 55.7 (89.6 km)

Unremarkable, little used station in southern San Jose. Similar to Capitol.

Blossom Hill is another station with just one platform.

A pair of simple bus stop-like shelters provides the only protection for waiting passengers.

Morgan Hill

17300 Depot Street, Morgan Hill, CA 95037
Opened: June 27, 1992
Mile Post 67.5 (108.6 km)

Martin Murphy established a ranch in this location in 1845. Part of the ranch was inherited by his granddaughter Diana who married a wealthy San Franciscan named Hiram Morgan Hill. In 1884, the Morgan Hills built a estate which they called "Villa Mira Monte."

A Southern Pacific Station was built at this location in 1898. SP referred to the station as Huntington (after Cornelius Huntington, the president of the Southern Pacific following Stanford's death). However, the locals referred to the stop as "Morgan Hill's Ranch."

A town by the name of Morgan Hill became incorporated November 10, 1906, and the SP changed the name of the stop to reflect local usage.

After World War II, and especially after 1970, Morgan Hill was rapidly suburbanized as many of the workers from the new silicon valley high tech firms flocked to the lower cost housing in southern Santa Clara County.

Right: A view of the original Morgan Hill station from the late nineteenth century.

Below: "Waiting For The Train" , a sculpture by Marlene Amerian at the station represents Hiram & Diana Morgan Hill waiting for a train with their young daughter.

Courtesy of Morgan Hill Historical Society

The city built a small post-modern station house after Caltrain was extended. A small coffee & snack counter occupies the building

Passengers disembark from a south-bound train.

A small snack bar sells coffee and pastries to commuters in the mornings

San Martin

South of Morgan Hill suburbia thins out and the countryside becomes increasingly rural. Garlic, mushrooms and fruit are major crops in this area. Between Morgan Hill and Gilroy is the unincorporated community of San Martin with a population of aprox. 4,000 people. San Martin has a simple Caltrain station with a single platform and simple prefabricated shelters.

Platform at San Martin.

Simple bus-stop like shelters at San Martin.

Above & below: Farmland still lines the tracks between San Martin and Gilroy.

The last train on a summer's evening in 2010 heads towards Gilroy.

Gilroy

7150 Monterey Street, Gilroy, Ca, 95020
Opened: 1869, Closed : May 1, 1971
Re-opened: June 27, 1992
Mile Post 77.4 (124.5 km)

Gilroy lies at the southern end of the Santa Clara Valley; where small Mexican village existed before the coming of the railroad. The present town was established when the original Southern Pacific Railroad reached this area in the late 1860's. The town was named after John Gilroy, a Scotsman who settled in the area in 1814. On March 12, 1870, the town was incorporated.

Gilroy calls itself the "Garlic Capital of the World." While Gilroy does not lead the world in garlic production, it does lead the world in garlic processing. The Gilroy Garlic Festival has been held each summer since 1979. Caltrain's first service extension were the special Garlic Festival trains in the 1980's.

The historic Southern Pacific depot (now a Greyhound bus station) is next to the Caltrain station at 7250 Monterey St. It is a reinforced concrete building that opened in 1918. At the time it was described by local newspapers as the most beautiful depot between San Francisco and Santa Barbara. It is an eclectic mix of Mission Revival, Roman and early twentieth century commercial architecture. The building was built on the southern edge of Gilroy's historic commercial district.

Gilroy had train service until the Del Monte regional service between San Francisco and Monterey was abandoned and the passenger station was closed on May 1, 1971. The station building was used for SP offices until 1985, when SP vacated the building. The Greyhound company later occupied the structure. The Coast Starlighter passes through Gilroy but does not stop here.

Above: Former Southern Pacific station at Gilroy, now used as a Greyhound bus station (Amtrak trains don't stop here, but Amtrak Through-Way buses do). The new Caltrain stop is just to the south of the old station

Right: A shelter for Caltrain passengers; its color and architecture is reminiscent of the former SP station.

Above: One of 3 trains held overnight at Gilroy for morning departure to San Francisco.

Right: The interior of the Gilroy train station, now used as a ticket office and waiting room for Greyhound buses. Note the craftsman style gold-leaf at the ceiling.

Below: An old SP departure board, now covered with Plexiglas. Note that south bound is referred to as "east bound" and north bound is referred to as "west bound". For safety reasons all trains heading towards San Francisco are officially referred to as west bound and all trains heading away are referred to as east bound, regardless of compass direction.

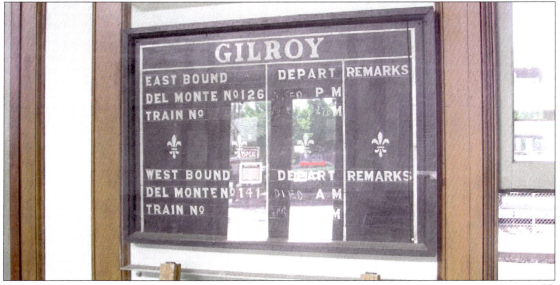

Made in the USA
San Bernardino, CA
10 April 2019